Crime and Punishment
Through the Ages

Written by Grant Bage
Illustrated by Martin Bustamante

Contents

Collins

T0321632

Introduction

If you go to school, you're probably an expert in rules. Every school has them, and you have to follow them. Families, clubs, games and gangs have rules, too. If you don't follow the rules you expect to be told off.

The story of crime and punishment is the story of society's rules, which we call laws. Laws have brought people pain, revenge, a new start or a terrible death. Through its laws, society works out what kind of punishment fits each crime.

a highway robbery 200 years ago

punishing a criminal 600 years ago

But what do the words "crime" and "punishment" mean?

A crime is something that seems wrong to groups of people who live or work together.

Punishment means what those people decide to do to others who commit crimes – either to stop them doing it again or to prevent others from copying them.

Our focus is stories of real crime and punishment over the last 2,000 years, from the place we now call Britain.

We'll also be looking at *how* and *why* crimes and punishments have changed or stayed the same over time. One special thing about history is that its stories need to be true. Historians take scraps of real evidence surviving from the past, like documents, objects, pictures or buildings. They then stitch this evidence together to work out what life was like in different ages, and what we can learn from those past lives.

a historian looks for evidence

4

mothers and children in a Victorian prison

2,000 years is a very long time for evidence to survive, so it's hard to tell exactly what happened in the distant past. For crime and punishment, evidence normally comes from the people who had the money and power to make the laws. Criminals, or the victims of criminals, rarely had the time or education to tell their stories – poor people, women and children, in particular.

Yet if you know where to look, the stories of these people can be found. You'll find some of them here.

What do they show and what do they mean? Well, that's now up to you to decide.

The Romans

Crime costs more than money: it causes suffering and trouble for victims. When crime happens today, people generally call the police. What about in Roman Britain?

In Roman times (the 1st to the 4th century CE), Britain was part of the Roman **Empire**. Rome was the Empire's capital city. From Rome, the Empire stretched about a thousand kilometres in each direction. Over such a huge area, it was difficult to control crime effectively. So when somebody stole from Honoratus, a man living in Western England in about 200 CE, there wasn't a police force to contact. In those days, victims had to find and **prosecute** criminals themselves.

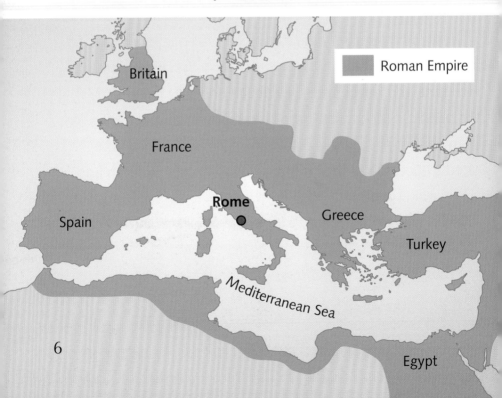

Britain

Roman Empire

France

Spain

Rome

Greece

Turkey

Mediterranean Sea

Egypt

Honoratus probably told a local Roman official about the theft, but he also visited a temple. Scratching a message on to a metal tablet, he cursed the thief and asked the gods for help:

HONORATUS, TO THE HOLY GOD MERCURY. I COMPLAIN THAT I HAVE LOST TWO WHEELS AND FOUR COWS AND MANY SMALL BELONGINGS FROM MY HOUSE. PLEASE ... DO NOT ALLOW HEALTH TO THE PERSON WHO HAS DONE ME WRONG .... WHETHER MAN OR WOMAN, BOY OR GIRL, ENSLAVED OR FREE, DO NOT ALLOW THE THIEF TO LIE OR SIT OR DRINK OR EAT UNLESS THE THIEF BRINGS MY PROPERTY TO ME.

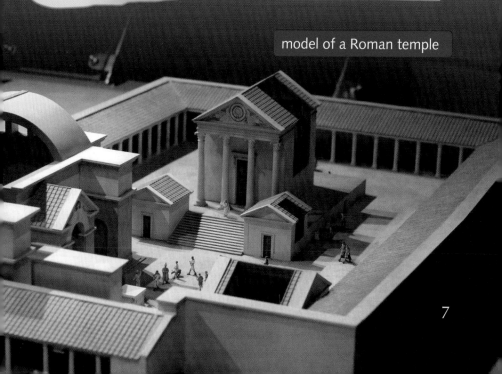

model of a Roman temple

7

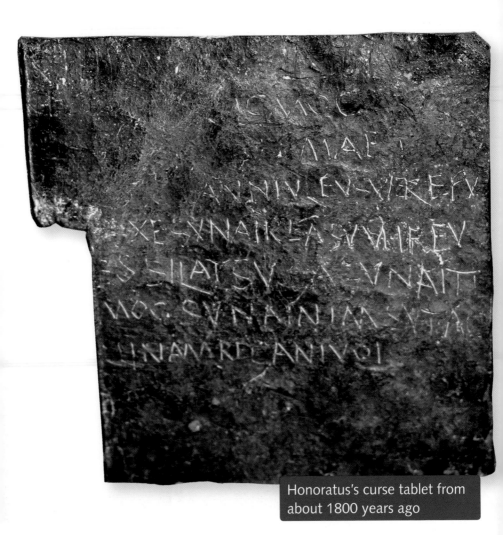

Honoratus's curse tablet from about 1800 years ago

Honoratus's message is called a "curse tablet". We'll never know whether Honoratus got his cows back, but archaeologists have dug up similar messages from men and women across Britain. So how were thieves punished, in Roman times?

Different laws for enslaved people and citizens

How Roman robbers were punished depended upon who they were.

People in the Roman Empire were citizens or enslaved. Citizens had more **rights** than enslaved people. A citizen caught stealing paid a **fine** worth four times what they had stolen. Or they were whipped and forced to work like an enslaved person for a short time.

For stealing, an enslaved person could be crucified. Crucifixion meant they were stripped; then nailed to a tree or cross. Hanging in that position **dislocated** their shoulders and elbows, causing great pain. It soon became hard to breathe, but it could take days to die.

A closer look at slavery

Enslaved people were enslaved for life, unless an owner set them free. Roman farms, factories and cities were powered by enslaved people. Enslaved people of any age could be captured in war, and then sold in a marketplace. Sometimes desperate, poor families also sold their own children into slavery to help feed the rest of the family. Enslaved people outnumbered owners, and perhaps that's why Roman laws to control them were so harsh. If an owner hurt or killed an enslaved person, it wasn't considered a crime. But when an enslaved person did even a small thing wrong, owners could either let them off or make the punishment brutal.

a modern picture of a Roman market to buy and sell enslaved people

Did you know?

In 73 BCE, Spartacus led an army of fellow enslaved people to fight for freedom. After Spartacus was defeated, 6,000 enslaved people were crucified. Their bodies lined 200 kilometres of the main road into Rome. It was a warning to other enslaved people: never disobey Roman laws.

Enslaved people punished for rebelling

Laws about everything

Old documents show the city of Rome had courts and lawyers to deal with people who broke the law, but little written evidence survives to show exactly how justice was carried out in Roman Britain. However, we can get some idea about law and order in Britain at this time by looking at Roman laws.

a Roman court at work

Julius Caesar was a great Roman politician and general, who was born in 100 BCE. He was a famous soldier, who conquered Gaul (France) and briefly invaded southern England. But because he wanted to be emperor, Caesar needed detailed laws to help him create a strong government in Rome and beyond. Laws were important because they helped everyday life to run smoothly, in all parts of the Empire. That's why Caesar spent a lot of time making laws about everyday things, such as ditches, fences, pavements and street-cleaning, as well as big events such as elections, public games and circuses. Although many of these laws were about life in the vast city of Rome, some of them would have shaped life in Britain too.

Did you know?

Skeletons of beheaded bodies have been dug up from Roman cemeteries across England. Criminals, perhaps, killed for law-breaking?

Anglo-Saxons and Vikings

The Romans ruled Britain for around 400 years.
Roman soldiers finally left Britain in 410 CE, as the western
part of the Roman Empire broke slowly into smaller kingdoms
and tribes. The Anglo-Saxon period lasted from the end
of Roman Britain until the arrival of the Normans in 1066.
Historians used to call this time "the Dark Ages", partly
because law and order seemed to vanish: but perhaps laws
just changed, rather than disappearing completely?

King Ethelbert

Laws about fighting

At first, after the Romans, none of the new kingdoms seemed to last long enough for clear laws to be agreed and written down. Then around 610 CE, over 1,400 years ago, 90 written laws appear from King Aethelbert of Kent. Most of them were about fighting.

> Law 33   For seizing a man by the hair 50 silver pennies shall be paid as **compensation**.
>
> Law 50   He who smashes a chin bone shall pay for it with 20 shillings.
>
> Law 51   For each of the four front teeth, six shillings shall be paid as compensation.

These were not punishments to prevent fighting; they were payments between people to make peace, after fights had happened. Only about 25 of Aethelbert's laws mentioned women, children or enslaved people.

> Law 77   If a man buys a **maiden** the bargain shall stand, if there is no dishonesty.
>
> Law 79   If she wishes to depart with her children, she shall have half the goods.
>
> Law 89   The sum to be paid for robbing an enslaved person on the highway shall be three shillings.

Keeping the peace

King Aethelbert had two difficult jobs. The first was to win battles. After the Romans left Britain, there were countless Celtic, Anglo-Saxon and later Viking tribes fighting each other for land, treasure and enslaved people.

Aethelbert's second job was to "keep the peace" inside his little kingdom in Kent. As his laws show, people were expected to settle arguments themselves by paying each other money. Even killing somebody had a price, not a punishment. "Wergeld" was the price paid to the dead person's family, by those who had killed their relative.

Law 22   If one man kills another he shall pay 20 shillings Wergeld before the grave is closed … and 80 shillings within 40 days.

But harsh punishments were introduced for anybody who didn't pay the Wergeld compensation. For example, about 80 years later, King Ine of Wessex decreed:

King Egbert

> Law 12   If a thief is taken he shall die the death unless he pays his Wergeld.

If he (or she) was a lucky thief they might escape death by being enslaved. But:

> Law 24   ... If somebody being punished as an enslaved person runs away, they shall be hanged.

King Ine had one even simpler way to control thieves:

> Law 37   If a common person has often been accused of theft and is at last caught in the act of committing an offence ... a hand or foot shall be cut off.

Trial by ordeal

In Anglo-Saxon times, kings and queens promised three things, as the crowns were placed upon their heads: to keep the peace, to stop robbery and wrongdoing, and to be fair. They also wanted to be powerful, and in those days a lot of power was tied up with the Christian church. So kings like Aethelbert and Ine often asked Christian priests to write laws for them.

the coronation of King Harold

Priests had also invented a new method to decide whether someone accused of a crime was innocent or guilty: "the ordeal". If a killing or crime couldn't be settled by payment, or if somebody seemed to be lying, priests were called in. They blessed a pot of water, heated it over a fire and dropped a stone or lump of iron into it. The accused person said out loud that they were innocent, and then plunged their arm into the boiling water to pull out the object. If the burns on their hand and arm were clean after three days, the priests said this proved they were innocent. If the wounds became yellow and infected, it meant they were guilty.

an accused man about to go through the ordeal

19

Oath-bearers

Although the ordeal was painful and difficult, it wasn't meant to be a punishment – it was mostly a way of trying to work out if someone was guilty or innocent. Another, slightly easier way of doing this was to ask local people called oath-bearers their opinion of the people involved in a crime.

Oath-bearers made a solemn promise about whether the accused, or the person accusing them, could be trusted. The idea was that in most towns and villages at the time, everybody knew everybody else – so an honest person would attract more oath-bearers on their side than somebody spiteful or untruthful.

Justice and punishment

In Britain, courts were first used to decide about cases in Anglo-Saxon times. There were several different types of court. The king sometimes judged important crimes, from courts in London or other big cities, but there were also shire courts in country areas, and smaller village courts. In some village courts, the local landowner was the judge, punishing enslaved people at will by whipping, **mutilating** or hanging them. But free people could always ask the king for justice. Of course, the king couldn't judge every case, all across the country, and so each shire court had a paid **sheriff** who worked for the king. Free people could seek justice at these shire courts, where the sheriffs organised oath-bearers, Wergeld payments, and many sorts of punishments including hanging people.

Did you know?

Today police, lawyers and evidence help decide on crimes and punishments. Yet promises to tell the truth are still made in courts, as they were over 1,000 years ago. As England's most famous Anglo-Saxon king, Alfred, laid down in his laws:

Law 1 In the first place ... as a matter of supreme importance ... every man shall keep carefully to his oath.

The Normans

The Anglo-Saxon kings and queens ruled England until 1066, when the famous king, William the Conqueror, won the Battle of Hastings. William came from Normandy in France, and through that battle gained power over England (though not most of Wales, Scotland or Ireland).

William's victory meant he could seize land, collect taxes, build castles and pay armies. William became king through having enough skill, money and greed to fight to the death for power. So what did William's arrival change?

William the Conqueror

Did you know?

Imprisonment was a punishment that Anglo-Saxons and Vikings rarely used. Because their buildings were mostly small and wooden, they could not easily contain prisoners.

Castles and prisons

Some things changed a lot. Enslaving local people to work, the Normans quickly built wooden castles in every large town. These castles showed everyone that the Normans were in charge. Many castles were later rebuilt in stone, and then came to be used as prisons. For example, the Tower of London was first built in wood, and then rebuilt in stone in about 1078. During the next 500 years and more, rich or dangerous prisoners who challenged the law were locked up inside its walls, and often beheaded in front of each other. The Tower of London still stands today.

Local castles were used as prisons during Norman times too. There were no fixed rules about which crimes people could be imprisoned for, or for how long – it often depended on people's wealth whether they were hanged, mutilated, or only put in prison.

the Tower of London

Prison as punishment

To be locked up inside a Norman castle must have been frightening; the Normans didn't always treat their enemies well. Imprisonment was kinder than being hanged or beheaded, but also a lot more expensive; so it was a punishment generally used only for rich people. William the Conqueror even imprisoned his own half-brother, Odo – the Bishop of Bayeux, in Normandy.

Bishop Odo

24

Bishop Odo's prison cell may have looked like this.

William gave Odo lots of English land after the conquest, even leaving Odo in charge when he went fighting in France. Yet Odo was greedy for more, and unlawfully seized church treasures and land. When William returned in 1082, he was angry. William shouted at his brother in front of everybody: "It's never right to let off one man, against the general good." So William had Odo **arrested** as punishment and imprisoned in a French castle for four years.

A monk called Orderic wrote down Odo's story, about 40 years after it happened. Orderic ended with the words: "Odo lost everything and for years was very unhappy in prison ... an example for all young people." Orderic was trying to teach readers not just that William was a good king, but that crime would always be punished.

Pickpockets and punishments

Odo was lucky to be put in prison for his crimes.
It only happened because he was rich, powerful and
the king's brother. As the following story shows, it might take
a miracle to stop a common thief being hanged.

In the year 1080, a crowd had
gathered in Oxford to worship
a saint called Egwin.
Egwin had died 400
years before but people
believed his bones could
still perform miracles.
A woman in the crowd
brought money in
a purse, to offer the saint.
Little did she know that,
twice, a pickpocket sneaked
his hand in her purse and
slipped out pennies. But on the third

Saint Egwin

time, the thief's hand froze. He couldn't move it! People in
the crowd spotted what was happening, seized the thief
and were soon getting ready to hang him. But Saint Egwin's
monks prayed so hard the crowd changed their minds.
They forgave the pickpocket.

"Saint Egwin performed two miracles that day," wrote
Dominic the monk, "by saving the woman from theft … and
mercifully saving the thief from death."

Like the monk who wrote down this story, William
the Conqueror also disapproved of hanging criminals for
most crimes. William preferred other punishments: prison
for the rich, or chopping off poorer criminals' hands or feet.
For different crimes, Norman law also now allowed the slicing
off of ears, the poking out of eyes and the cutting off
of noses. The thief in this story had a very lucky escape!

Forest Laws

Like Anglo-Saxon kings before him, William the Conqueror's favourite hobby was hunting wild animals. But to keep the best hunting to themselves, the Normans made new rules called "Forest Laws".

Forest Laws covered one third of England, changing everything for people already living in the woods, forests and pastures. The laws banned families from catching hare, wild boar or deer. Only the king and his servants were allowed to hunt those animals. Blinding, chopping off hands or hanging were punishments for disobedience.

People living under Forest Laws were also not allowed to cut down trees to make houses, to put up fences or gather firewood. If they broke those rules, they had to pay a fine as punishment. It became very hard to make a living.

When William died in 1087, a monk wrote of his "great wisdom and power ... William put his own brother in prison ... He kept good order in the land so any man could travel safely."

Yet the monk also complained that William "was sunk in greed ... He set apart a vast deer park ... whoever killed a deer was to be blinded. For he loved the stags as dearly as though he had been their father."

For better and worse, Norman laws changed many things. Yet 50 years later, those laws fell apart.

The Middle Ages

In the Middle Ages, kings made laws and punished people, but they lived in fear of others plotting against them. Sometimes the plotters were powerful landowners called barons, who were rich enough to hire their own soldiers. There were always some barons who liked the idea of being king.

King Henry I was the son of William the Conqueror. Henry had no sons, but the English barons had promised Henry his daughter Matilda could become queen when he died. The barons broke their promise. They disliked being ruled by a woman, and in 1135, they crowned Matilda's cousin Stephen as king.

Henry I

King Stephen

Queen Matilda

War followed, and law and order disappeared. In 1137, a monk wrote: "Barons filled the land with castles. Working men and women they threw into prison and tortured for gold and silver. One was hung up by the thumbs, another by the head ..."

Cruelty was now being used not to punish criminals and enforce laws, but to rob honest people.

So when Stephen died and Matilda's son became King Henry II in 1154, he changed everything. Sheriffs had existed since Anglo-Saxon times, but Henry now imprisoned sheriffs who did their job badly. He told each sheriff to get local people into a group (a **jury**). The juries listed recent crimes, and who they thought had committed them. Judges appointed by the king then visited each year, to decide punishments and check the law was working.

Juries and judges

This story from around 1175 shows the importance of Henry II's new idea about judges, who could check if local juries were working properly and making the right decisions.

Two women were charged with murder and put in prison in York, awaiting the king's judge to visit. One died before the judge arrived, so a local jury decided to put the other woman through the ordeal of hot iron, which involved holding and carrying a red-hot rod of iron. After three days a lump appeared on the woman's burnt hand, so the 12 men of the jury said she should be burnt alive, in public.

the ordeal of hot iron

Benedicuo ferri & migne.

We only know about this story because the king's judge then arrived. He found out the woman had run to church and prayed hard to Saint William, and the lump on her hand had disappeared. The judge then let her go and also fined each man on the jury, for making an unfair decision.

Public punishments

Punishments for crime were always made in the open, so everybody could see and learn from them. In London there was a small stream, at a place called Cheapside. Because houses then had no pipes or taps, this was a popular spot for families to fetch fresh water each day. In 1293, three men had their right hands cut off in public at Cheapside, for helping a prisoner to escape; everybody could watch.

Each parish also had a whipping post, to which people were tied and beaten publicly for less important offences.

Cheapside in about 1580

Prisoners' stories

Norwich had a Norman castle, which later became a prison. From 1307 to 1316, as the king had ordered, lists were made of prisoners waiting there for judgement. There were 777 different cases involving thousands of people, written on to rolls of thick paper. Amazingly, these documents have survived. Here are two of their stories:

Matilda the Miller and Cecilia were accused by Isabel Lither of stealing a coat, sheet, towel, hood and two sacks of grain. Isabel did not attend court and so will be arrested. Matilda is found not guilty, Cecilia is **convicted**. She is to be hanged.

John Munk stole a cow worth five shillings. Also he made false money and was arrested with **counterfeit** pennies. He is convicted. His guts are to be drawn out, then he is to be hanged. His wife Alice is acquitted.

Norwich Castle

These documents don't explain why people became criminals, although we know now that more crime happened when bread prices rose and people went hungry. Most judges and juries at this time showed little mercy to those who committed crimes because of hunger – though a jury in 1316 decided not to hang a thief called Peter who had only stolen because he was "hungry and homeless". They sent Peter back to prison while they made "more enquiries". Unfortunately, no further documents survive, so we'll never know what happened to Peter.

Outlaws

One of the most famous criminals of the Middle Ages may never have existed at all! Robin Hood was a legendary outlaw who – according to the stories – once lived in Sherwood Forest. Robin robbed the rich and gave their money to the poor.

We don't know if Robin Hood really existed, but other outlaws certainly did. "Outlawing" was used as a punishment for crimes from Anglo-Saxon times until 1328. People named as outlaws were outside the protection of the law, which meant they could lawfully be killed by anybody, without warning. Outlaws lived in constant fear.

an artist's impression of Robin Hood and his men

The Peasants' Revolt

Outlaws lived outside the law, but sometimes ordinary people rebelled against laws they thought were unfair. In 1381, in the reign of King Richard II, the government invented a new tax called the poll tax. This had to be paid by every adult. Armed tax collectors visited villages across England, bullying people into paying – but people rebelled. The rebels marched to London, where they attacked the homes and businesses of lords, bishops and lawyers. Eventually the rebel leader, Wat Tyler, was tricked and the revolt collapsed. Hundreds were hanged, and Tyler's body was chopped into pieces. But from then on, kings could never forget that unfair laws and taxes could lead to big trouble.

The Tudors and Stuarts

From 1485 to 1603, England, Wales and most of Ireland were ruled by five Tudor kings and queens – Henry VII, Henry VIII, Edward VI, Mary I and Elizabeth I. During this period their kingdom became a more peaceful and a wealthier place in general, but criminals continued to be hanged in public for crimes such as robbery, burglary and murder. There were also many other frightening punishments used to stop people from committing crime in the first place, such as whipping and **branding**. For example, in 1495, a law picked out "**vagabonds**" as dangerous, because they were "idle people living suspiciously". Nobody could see how vagabonds earned money, or where they lived, so people were suspicious of them and thought they should be punished. Tudor and Stuart people had no police force, telephones, radio, TV or internet. Vagabonds scared people because wild stories about them spread quickly, but vagabonds themselves were hard to track.

The punishment for being a vagabond was the same for men and women. The first-time punishment was being branded on one ear, tied to a cart and whipped "until the back was bloody". The second time, the vagabond's other ear was branded, the whipping was repeated and the vagabond was made to work. If caught a third time, the vagabond would be hanged.

At just one London court between 1572 and 1574, 44 vagabonds were whipped and five were hanged. These punishments were not for something bad, such as robbery or fighting. They were simply for committing the "crime" of being workless and homeless: for being a vagabond.

Pirates

Tudor law-makers disliked homeless vagabonds because it cost money to feed and shelter them. People were also frightened that vagabonds might steal things. But there could be mixed feelings about other criminals in Tudor times. For example, pirates were basically just robbers who travelled by ship, but stories from across England and Wales suggest they were sometimes quite liked.

pirates at their worst

Possibly that was because pirates sold stolen things cheaply to local people. One such pirate was John Piers, who lived with his mother Anne in the Cornish fishing town of Padstow. John was a pirate, and his mother helped him. In 1581, Anne was questioned. She admitted meeting her son at midnight, at Padstow harbour. He gave her a stolen rug which she carried with two friends to a nearby barn. Padstow's vicar said Anne received stolen metal plates and silver buttons, and sold stolen cloth to many people including another local vicar. A different witness told how John Piers gave her husband a cask of soap, two guns and a parrot.

But even if local people liked the pirates, the authorities often dealt with them harshly. John and 15 of his gang were arrested. Orders arrived from London to hang them, and leave their bodies to rot near the harbour. Although they escaped from Dorchester prison, John was soon recaptured. There was no escape this time, although history doesn't record what became of his mother.

Witchcraft

Robbery and violence by vagabonds or pirates were real dangers. People also had other, stranger fears. One was the crime of witchcraft. In Tudor and Stuart times, many people were frightened of being made ill, or their farm crops and animals being harmed, by witches with magical powers. Between 1500 and 1700 perhaps 4,000 people, mostly older women, were accused of witchcraft across Britain.

The ordeal of hot iron, an old way of testing guilt or innocence, was stopped by the church in 1215. Yet nearly 400 years later, witches were still being tried using the ordeal of water.

the ordeal of water

In 1611, in Northampton, England, Arthur Bill and his mother and father were arrested. The judges tied each of them thumb to toe, and threw them in the water. They floated, which showed their "guilt": of course, if they had been "innocent", they would have sunk and drowned anyway.

Arthur's mother cut her own throat; his father claimed Arthur was a witch and gave witness against him. Arthur was found guilty of harming cattle and murdering a woman with spells, and was hanged.

three witches being hanged

Sometimes "witches" were tortured to get them to confess. In 1592, in Edinburgh, Scotland, Agnes Tompson confessed under torture to keeping a toad, and using its poison to make James, King of Scotland, ill. The king himself questioned her. She was found guilty, strangled and then burnt.

Religion and punishment

In Tudor and Stuart times, people were sometimes imprisoned and punished because of their religious beliefs. Sometimes it was illegal to be a Catholic and sometimes it was illegal to be a Protestant.

In 1535, Henry VIII ordered Catholic monks to be tied to planks of wood and cut open. When his eldest daughter Mary became queen, over 200 Protestants were beheaded or burnt alive. Under her sister Queen Elizabeth I, Catholics were again imprisoned and executed.

Sometimes people were burned alive because of their beliefs.

Receiue my spirit.

44

In 1603, James, King of Scotland, became the king of England. Because James wouldn't allow Catholics to worship openly, a Catholic gang made a plan. In 1604, they rented a building near London's Houses of Parliament, and started a tunnel. By 4 November 1605 everything was ready. Cellars under Parliament were stacked with barrels of gunpowder. King James and his government would be blown up the next day.

King James

It never happened. Guy Fawkes was arrested in the cellars. King James signed an order and Fawkes was tortured.

Guy Fawkes

His punishment for **treason** was to be hanged, taken down still alive, his stomach cut open and the guts burnt before his eyes. However, Fawkes fell off the **scaffold** and broke his neck before that punishment began.

Did you know?

Bonfires and fireworks are still lit on 5 November in many parts of Britain. But people still don't agree. Was Guy Fawkes a terrorist – or a freedom fighter?

18th century

During the 18th century, kings and queens still had power and influence, but their laws were now made by politicians in the Houses of Parliament. From 1702 to 1714, the queen of England was Queen Anne, and as in previous times, public brandings, beheadings, burnings and hangings were still being used as punishments for serious crime. However, most criminals suffered less extreme punishments. For example, in 1701: "Mary Harris, a Black-woman of St Giles in the Fields … stole a pair of sheets, three smocks and other goods from Nicholas Laws, a gentleman." Mary was lucky. It was her first offence so she was sentenced only to a public whipping.

Queen Anne

Another common punishment at this time was the "stocks" – heavy pieces of wood or iron, hinged at one end and with holes for people's feet. Offenders sat on a bench for hours, their feet locked. To make them ashamed, their crime was announced to the watching crowd: perhaps they'd been drunk, sold rotten food or told lies.

The pillory was similar to the stocks, though the offender stood with their head and hands locked. Some unpopular offenders were even killed in the pillory, by stones thrown from the crowd.

Did you know?

Daniel Defoe, who wrote *Robinson Crusoe*, was put in the pillory for publishing an essay poking fun at churchmen. He was popular and lucky, and the crowd threw only flowers at him. Normally, it was rotten food, dead animals, mud and worse.

Women and the law

Throughout most of history, laws have been made and enforced by men. Men were the judges, law-makers and law-enforcers, yet in 1700 almost as many women as men were being put on trial at London's Old Bailey court. Over the next 100 years this changed. By 1800, only 22% of those appearing at this court were women. Because women's lives often centred more around the home, they perhaps had fewer opportunities than men to commit serious crimes. Men were also often thought to be stronger and more violent than women; so male criminals were more feared and more severely punished than women.

a woman appearing before the court

This didn't mean women were weak. For instance, 18th century documents from a London law court show Mrs Proctor and her two daughters being fined for beating up a law officer while trying to rescue a male relative.

Across Britain, women sometimes also broke the law to control local food prices. For example, in Taunton, Somerset, in 1753, several hundred women marched to the Town Mill and demolished it, to stop corn being milled, while men stood looking on and cheering. The women were cross with the mill manager for putting up the price of flour.

Transportation as a punishment

Transportation began to be used as a punishment in 1717. Criminals who were transported were taken by ship to a foreign land, and left there. At first they were taken to America, and then later to Australia. Seven out of eight criminals transported were men or boys – some as young as nine or ten. Transportation ended in 1868, by which time about 250,000 criminals had been sent abroad. Why was this punishment used so often?

transported convicts arriving in a new land

It was partly a matter of kindness, and partly cost. Transportation doesn't sound "kind". It was rare for convicts who were transported to see family, friends or home again. Yet for serious crimes, the law's only other punishment was death by hanging. For example, hanging was the punishment for theft, but most courts didn't want to hang petty thieves. However, if a crime had been committed, the criminal couldn't be let off. At least transportation kept criminals alive. If they worked hard in their new country, transportees might even make a better life for themselves.

18th-century prisons

Even though hanging and transportation were common punishments, there were still around 10,000 people in prison in the 1770s. Prisons ranged in size from tiny one-room lock-ups in villages to castle prisons in towns.

Many 18th-century prisoners were debtors – often business owners who couldn't pay their debts. The people they owed money to could take them to court, and they would have to stay in a debtors' prison until they paid up. Because prisoners had to pay to live in debtors' prisons, often they ended up owing even more money! This meant some debtors never got out of prison, unless family or friends paid off their debts for them.

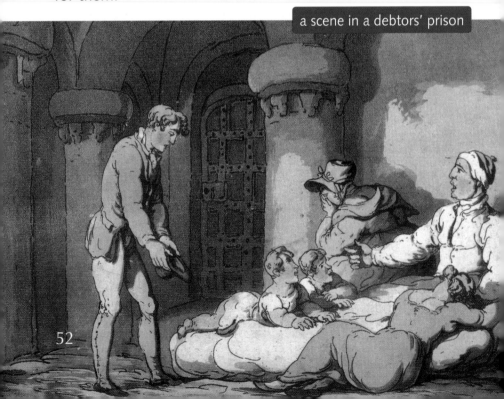

a scene in a debtors' prison

Richer people in debtors' prisons could have an easier time, with access to on-site restaurants and shops. But for poor people, the conditions could be terrible. Some debtors even starved to death.

The 18th-century campaigner John Howard was shocked by prison conditions and tried to persuade the government to change things. This is what he said about Durham prison in 1777:

"The men are put at night into dungeons. One is seven feet square for three prisoners. Another called the 'Great Hole' has only a little window. In this I saw six prisoners ... chained to the floor."

Campaigners like John Howard visited prisons to find out about the conditions.

19th century
Conditions in prison

In the 19th century, Elizabeth Fry, like John Howard, tried to make prisons better. She visited London's Newgate prison in 1812. Fry was shocked by female prisoners with babies, wearing ragged, filthy clothes and with no bedding to sleep on. Cells were shared and there was constant bullying, gambling and fighting. Fry wrote in February 1813 to her own children:

"I have lately been twice to Newgate to see the prisoners ... who had poor little infants without clothing, or with very little. If you saw how small a piece of bread they are each allowed a day you would be very sorry."

Elizabeth Fry

Elizabeth Fry visiting a prison

In 1819, Elizabeth and her brother Joseph visited prisons in Scotland. Their idea of a "good" prison was that a vicar, teacher and doctor visited often, and "prisoners during the day are constantly at work. Much attention is given to cleanliness – the prisoners have to wash often – a Bible is placed in every cell."

Riots over food prices

In 1700, about 8 million people lived in Britain. By 1850, it was over 27 million. Every extra mouth needed feeding and when food prices rose, families went hungry. Hunger could make even good, normally well-behaved people dangerous.

During May 1816, a crowd of men and women gathered in the small town of Brandon, Suffolk, demanding lower food prices. The local newspaper described the scene:

> They destroyed several houses including Mr Willett's the butcher. They were armed with long heavy sticks ... the ends studded with short iron spikes, sharp at the sides and points. On their flag was written "Bread or Blood".

People in towns and cities rioted over the price of food.

Similar things happened in other towns nearby. In Littleport, the local vicar ran away, after crowds smashed up and looted his house. Men and women "had armed themselves with dangerous and offensive weapons ... bludgeons, pitchforks, iron spikes and guns".

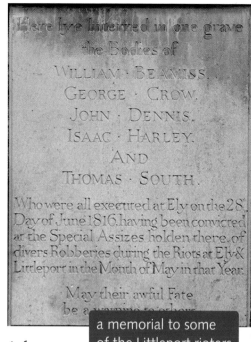

a memorial to some of the Littleport rioters

The army was called in. A farm worker was shot dead, a soldier lost his arm and over 50 people were arrested. Others ran away.

One of the Littleport rioters wrote to his wife from London.

Mak your self as esy as Yu can for I shall not take any hurt...

Like many others, this man was soon caught again. He was lucky, ending up only in prison. His friends were mostly transported, or hanged.

Hanging

During this time, punishments were getting tougher. In 1688, there were 50 different "hanging crimes", for which people could be hanged. By 1765 it was 160. By 1815 it was over 200. Hanging crimes included breaking into houses, or stealing animals. Law-makers hoped the threat of execution, even for small crimes, would stop crime happening.

After the 1816 Littleport riots, 24 people were told they would hang. The court had no choice, because the laws said even those who had only stolen food, or thrown stones at the soldiers, should die. Then followed long arguments about who deserved "mercy". Finally, only five of the rioters were hanged.

a criminal about to be hanged

58

Racist attitudes were common in Britain at this time. For example, in 1819, 15-year-old Henry Lovell was hanged outside Newgate prison. His victim said in court: "A number of boys jumped over a hedge. The prisoner knocked my hat off. I struck him. He cried out 'cut his throat!' Near 50 of them came up. I was beat about every part of my body. I lost a silver snuff-box, 16 shillings in money, a pair of gloves, and a silk handkerchief."

A witness called Sarah Thomas knew Henry Lovell, and in her evidence she mentioned that he was a Gipsy and dark skinned. This might explain why, from a gang of 50, only Henry was charged and hanged.

Changing attitudes to crime

Although it was too late to save Henry
Lovell, things were changing.
In 1818–19 "select committees"
from the Houses of Parliament
researched all the crimes that
could end in hanging, and heard
from Elizabeth Fry about prisons.

Sir Robert Peel

These committees helped
a politician called Robert Peel
to make gradual changes in crime
and punishment. Between 1823 and 1830 Parliament voted
"yes" to:

- making British laws and punishments simpler and fairer
- paying for more, better organised and healthier prisons
- proper police forces, starting in London.

an early photograph of policemen

60

Did you know?
• •

In the 1700s, especially in London, "thief takers" made money by catching criminals and claiming rewards. The richest and most famous was Jonathan Wild. Yet Wild secretly led a criminal gang, buying and selling stolen property. In 1725, Wild was hanged.

The police

Ideas for a better "police force" had been around since the 1700s. They became real in 1829 when Metropolitan Police constables started work in London. Unlike watchmen, constables or thief takers, who had done similar jobs before, these were professional policemen, in uniform. More importantly, they were paid by the government, not by rewards, just to stop crime and catch criminals.

Ways of tackling crime and punishment were changing. And over the next 30 years, every part of Britain developed a similar police force.

policemen about to arrest a suspect

61

Changing punishments

During the 19th century, some punishments became less severe. It became less common for even persistent thieves to be hanged. For example, 16-year-old thief Michael Nagle appeared "again" at the Old Bailey in September 1847 for stealing a watch. Britain now had a police force, and a policeman told the court about Michael's earlier imprisonment for theft. Michael's defence was that the stolen watch "was given to me to sell by a bigger boy than myself".

a policeman from about 125 years ago

This time, Michael was imprisoned for one year, and publicly whipped. Although this seems harsh, he was lucky in a way: 30 years earlier, Michael would have been hanged.

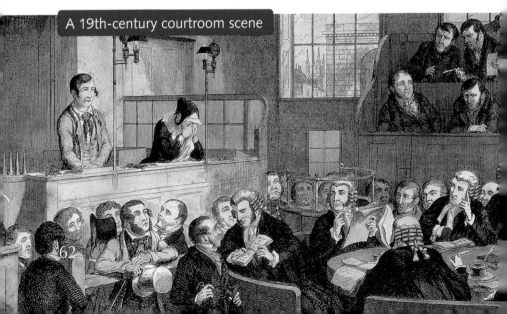

A 19th-century courtroom scene

Hanging was still a common punishment for murder, however. For instance, Catherine Foster was only 17 years old in 1847, when she was hanged for poisoning her husband. 10,000 people gathered in Suffolk to watch her

being hanged. It had become traditional for criminals to make a speech from the scaffold. Catherine warned her listeners to keep their marriage vows. Local newspapers printed detailed reports of the hanging, and Catherine, like many other criminals, became more famous through death than she ever was in life.

Science and crime-solving

In 1868, British law changed so that people could no longer be hanged in public. Hangings now took place privately, inside prison. Fighting crime was becoming less about public punishments and demonstrations of cruelty, and more about using the police, science and information to solve crimes.

Here's an example from 1886. Mary Britland's 19-year-old daughter died, and Mary claimed ten pounds in life insurance. Then Mary's husband died, and she claimed a further ten pounds. Feeling sorry for Mary, her neighbour invited her to stay – and then she too fell ill and died. Friends contacted the police, and all three bodies were dug up. Scientific examination showed poison in their stomachs. Mary had bought similar poison from the chemist, explaining "my house has mice".

Mary Britland

During the later years of the 19th century, the science of **forensics** became more and more important. Scientific tests were developed to show the presence of blood at crime scenes, and photographs began to be used as evidence in trials. In 1880, a Scotsman called Henry Faulds developed a way to use fingerprints to solve crime. All these aspects of forensics, and many more, are still used for crime-fighting today.

Henry Faulds

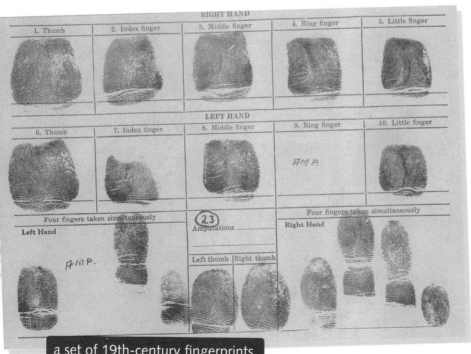

a set of 19th-century fingerprints

20th century

Women changing the law

Female criminals were often treated more kindly than men, but it was men who judged them. Women in 1900 didn't enforce or make laws. It was 1915 before Britain had its first policewoman. By 1939, only a quarter of English and Welsh police forces had policewomen.

For a thousand years, juries of local people had helped decide criminals' guilt or innocence. Yet before 1920 juries had no women. Britain's first female judge wasn't appointed until 1956.

Rose Heilbron, the first female judge

some of the first policewomen

WOMEN PO
SERVIC

In 1904, some British women started to protest. Women couldn't vote in elections to Parliament, which made new laws. Why, when over half of men could

> ### Did you know?
> In prison, some suffragettes starved themselves, so food was forced down their throats. That was painful and dangerous.

vote? Parliament refused to listen so "suffragettes" chained themselves to buildings, broke windows and refused to pay fines. By 1913, over 1,000 had been jailed.

From 1914 to 1918, the First World War raged. Suffragettes stopped their protests. Many did "male" jobs such as policing, whilst men were away fighting. Then when peace came, Parliament gave some women the vote. People still disagree about whether suffragette law-breaking changed men's minds, or whether it was because women did their wartime jobs so well.

Using different punishments

Although women in the early 20th century had little power or influence within the law, sometimes they were treated with understanding by the male judges. For example, Marie Corbett was arrested in 1900 when a policeman spotted her stealing the purse of an old lady on London's Liverpool Street railway station. The old lady was confused, and may have been drunk. Hearing that Marie had 13 children, and her husband was earning no money after an accident, the judge sentenced her to one day in prison for theft. Perhaps he thought the shame of prison was punishment enough?

In 1800, Marie could have been hanged, transported to Australia or publicly flogged.

By 1900, some punishments had changed, but the most serious punishment had not. That year an American called Hawley Crippen moved to London. Crippen claimed to be a doctor. In 1910, Crippen's wife disappeared, and his girlfriend moved in. Friends became suspicious and called the police, who searched his house. They found nothing, but soon after, Crippen rushed to catch a ship to Canada. The police searched his house again. Body parts were buried in the cellar! Scientific tests showed poison in them. Meanwhile, the ship's captain used a new invention, the radio, to alert police back in London. When the ship reached Canada, Crippen was arrested. His girlfriend was with him, disguised as a young man.

Four months later, Crippen was hanged.

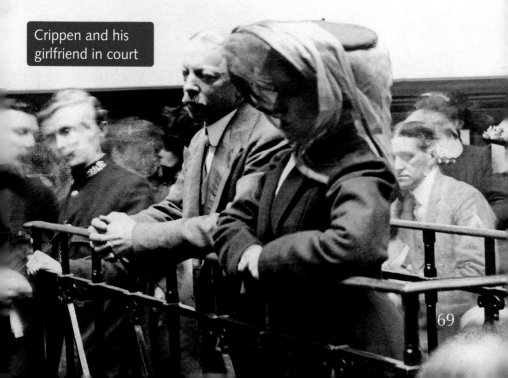

Crippen and his girlfriend in court

Everything speeds up

Petrol cars were invented in the 1880s, and in 1896 the first
British car driver was fined for speeding. Walter Arnold
was driving at 13 kilometres per hour, when caught by
a policeman on a bicycle! The speed limit at this time was
just three kilometres per hour in towns and villages, and six
kilometres per hour in the open countryside.

As cars became cheaper, British roads grew crowded
and dangerous. By 1930, all police forces had "motor patrols"
of cars and motorcycles, to help control speeding traffic, but
cars, buses and trucks still killed 30 children a week. In 1935,
over 200,000 people were injured in motor accidents,
and driving tests for new drivers became law. By 1965,
police had another road safety weapon:
a "magic eye" to photograph vehicles
breaking motorway speed limits.
Despite thousands of speed cameras
on today's British roads, speeding is
still the most common crime.

an early car

Criminals learnt quickly how to use cars for crimes. In 1935, a young woman in Hull, walking with a wage bag full of cash, was snatched by "motor bandits". They drove fast for several kilometres, whilst cutting chains securing the bag to her belt. Then they stopped, threw her out and sped away.

Thieves also learnt to steal cars, almost as soon as they were invented. In 1991, one British car was stolen, on average, every minute of every day. If parked in line, they would stretch from Cornwall to Scotland!

Children, corporal punishment and criminals

For most of history, when children did something seriously wrong, they were smacked by parents, teachers or police. Adults claimed that hurting children, just a little, taught them right from wrong. This was called corporal punishment. From 1933, boys and girls aged over ten who committed crimes could be sent to "approved schools". This might be for bad crimes, or for less serious ones like stealing coal or shoplifting. Going to an approved school was meant to teach useful new skills like gardening, bricklaying or cooking. Children lived in the school, often in remote areas far from home. Punishments for running away were strict: eight lashes with a cane – on the buttocks for boys and the hands for girls.

in the past, schoolchildren were often punished severely

the Staffordshire school where the gun theft took place

In 1947, nine teenaged boys from a Staffordshire approved school broke into a shed and stole guns. They killed a member of staff. Their plan was to murder the head teacher. After an enquiry, he was sacked, the school was shut and several boys were sent to prison.

In 1973, approved schools were changed to become "children's homes". By 2000, all British schools had been banned by law from using corporal punishment.

Crime and punishment then and now

As this book shows, stealing things, damaging property, telling lies to make money and hurting or killing other people have been common crimes for 2,000 years. What has changed most is how they are punished.

prisoners in a prison yard about 150 years ago

For example, in 1969, the British Parliament voted to stop hanging murderers, instead sending them to prison for the rest of their lives. The crime stayed the same, the punishment changed.

Similarly, in the past, British criminals might have been whipped, branded, burnt or blinded. But today we use prison and not physical pain, as a punishment for most serious crimes.

in a modern prison cell

In 1969, the internet was invented. The worldwide web followed in 1989. Computers and mobile phones are now common, cheap and used by most families. Yet criminals also use them to steal money, tell lies, threaten people and buy or sell stolen property.

Two hundred years ago, police officers walked the streets to catch criminals. Now they track crime on the internet and use hidden cameras to film dangerous driving, thefts from shops and criminals damaging property or picking fights.

In 1969, there were 40,000 prisoners in British jails; in 2009, more than 85,000. 50 years from now, technology may even have found a different way to punish criminals – maybe then, *nobody* will be locked up in jail?

Glossary

arrested   seized and put in prison

branding   burning with a hot iron

compensation   money given to someone who has suffered because of someone else's fault

convicted   found guilty by a court

counterfeit   false or fake

dislocated   put out of joint

empire   a number of different countries ruled over by one ruler or government

executions   killings carried out as punishments; hanging is one method

fine   money paid to make up for a crime

forensics   scientific tests used to help solve crimes

jury   a group of (usually) 12 people who decide whether someone accused of a crime is innocent or guilty

maiden   unmarried girl or woman

mutilating   cutting off or damaging parts of the body

prosecute   take a person to court

rights   things that a person is entitled to by law

scaffold   a raised wooden platform where criminals were hanged or beheaded

sheriff   a person responsible for justice in an area

treason   the crime of betraying the king, queen or country

vagabonds   people with no fixed home or job

Index

Changes in crime and punishment

Roman times
- No police force; people had to try to solve crimes for themselves.
- Different punishments for enslaved people and citizens.

Normans
- Wrongdoers imprisoned in castles – especially if rich.
- Poorer criminals could be mutilated or hanged.

Anglo-Saxons and Vikings
- If you committed crimes, you had to pay Wergeld.
- Thieves could have a hand or foot cut off.
- Courts and sheriffs made make sure justice was done.

Middle Ages
- Juries and judges appointed; trials became fairer.
- Criminals could be mutilated or hanged.

Tudors and Stuarts

- Criminals still hanged for robbery and murder, and could also be whipped, mutilated or branded.
- People accused of witchcraft were hanged or burnt if found guilty.

20th century

- Women first became judges and police officers.
- Hanging still the punishment for murder until 1969.
- Car crime began.

19th century

- Prison conditions became better.
- By the end of the century, hanging became less common.
- The police force started.
- Crime-solving became more scientific.

18th century

- Branding, beheading and hanging were used for serious crime; whipping, stocks and pillory for smaller crimes.
- Transportation became used as a punishment.
- Prison conditions often very bad.

21st century

- Prison, not physical pain or death, is used as a punishment.
- Computer crime common.

Ideas for reading

Written by Clare Dowdall, PhD
Lecturer and Primary Literacy Consultant

Reading objectives
- make comparisons within and across books
- draw inferences and justify these with evidence
- summarise the main ideas drawn from more than one paragraph, identifying key details that support the main ideas
- distinguish between statements of fact and opinion
- provide reasoned justifications for their views

Spoken language objectives:
- participate in discussions, presentations, performances, role play, improvisations and debates

Curriculum links: History – social history (Romans, Anglo-Saxons, Middle Ages)

Resources: Whiteboards, pens and paper

Build a context for reading
- Ask children to explain what the words "crime" and "punishment" mean. Can children name any famous criminals from history? (Be aware of individual children's circumstances.)
- Discuss how criminals were punished in the past, and whether children think these punishments were fair.
- Look at the cover and read the blurb. Ask children to predict which age contained the most harsh punishments for crime, and the most unfair treatment of the poor.

Understand and apply reading strategies
- Turn to pp2–3. Challenge children to quickly find a definition for a crime and punishment and share their ideas.
- Ask children to read pp4–5. Based on this reading, support children to make inferences about the accuracy of historical accounts, e.g. how the perspectives of the rich and educated were more widely preserved.